GUIDES TO RESPONSIBLE HUNTING
TRACKING AND HUNTING YOUR PREY

GUIDES TO RESPONSIBLE HUNTING

HUNTING ARMS

HUNTING SAFETY, LICENSING, AND RULES

PREPARING AND ENJOYING A MEAL YOU HUNTED

PREPARING FOR YOUR HUNTING TRIP

TRACKING AND HUNTING YOUR PREY

GUIDES TO RESPONSIBLE HUNTING
TRACKING AND HUNTING YOUR PREY

By Elizabeth Dee

MASON CREST

Mason Crest
450 Parkway Drive, Suite D
Broomall, Pennsylvania 19008
(866) MCP-BOOK (toll-free)
www.masoncrest.com

First printing
9 8 7 6 5 4 3 2 1

ISBN (hardback) 978-1-4222-4102-8
ISBN (series) 978-1-4222-4097-7
ISBN (ebook) 978-1-4222-7701-0

Cataloging-in-Publication Data on file with the Library of Congress

Developed and Produced by National Highlights Inc.
Editor: Keri De Deo
Interior and cover design: Priceless Digital Media
Production: Michelle Luke

CONTENTS

KEY ICONS TO LOOK FOR:

 Words to Understand: These words with their easy-to-understand definitions will increase the reader's understanding of the text while building vocabulary skills.

 Sidebars: This boxed material within the main text allows readers to build knowledge, gain insights, explore possibilities, and broaden their perspectives by weaving together additional information to provide realistic and holistic perspectives.

 Educational Videos: Readers can view videos by scanning our QR codes, providing them with additional educational content to supplement the text. Examples include news coverage, moments in history, speeches, iconic sports moments, and much more!

 Text-Dependent Questions: These questions send the reader back to the text for more careful attention to the evidence presented there.

 Research Projects: Readers are pointed toward areas of further inquiry connected to each chapter. Suggestions are provided for projects that encourage deeper research and analysis.

 Series Glossary of Key Terms: This back-of-the book glossary contains terminology used throughout this series. Words found here increase the reader's ability to read and comprehend higher-level books and articles in this field.

 Words to Understand:

dreys: Squirrel nests in the high branches of a tree.

scat: Animal feces or droppings.

spoor: Signs an animal makes when in an area, such as hoof tracks or devoured vegetation.

CHAPTER 1
ANIMAL SIGNS

LEARNING ABOUT ANIMALS AND THEIR HABITATS

Being a successful hunter is all about knowing how to discover the favorite habitats of wild animals. Knowing where a particular animal likes to live and raise their young and why they choose specific locations will help you locate more prey to hunt. Knowing how to recognize animal signs or **spoor** is the key to this knowledge.

You must know how to find your prey in the deep forest.

In this chapter, we will cover the spoor of the more common type for the young hunter to learn. As your skill level increases over time, you will be able to hunt more challenging game, such as a large elk.

What animals can you track in your location? Ask an experienced hunter before you start. Going into the wild with an adult can prove very valuable when learning the subtler points of how to track animals, but here are some fast facts to get you started.

Tracking 101
- Black Scout
Tutorials

WHAT YOU NEED TO KNOW ABOUT RABBITS

Rabbits provide a staple food source for many other animals. Young rabbits learn shortly after birth what it's like to be prey. These shy creatures are a good starter animal for the most inexperienced hunter because rabbits are timid creatures and don't pose a danger during the hunt like larger, fierce animals. However, after shooting a rabbit, make sure it is dead before picking it up because they can bite and kick.

Rabbits are lightning-fast runners and know quite a few tricks to discourage a hunter. One trick a wild rabbit will use is to run through thorny bushes and clumps of briars where it's difficult or painful for you to follow. Another trick they typically use is to run in a zigzag pattern that makes it hard to get a good shot.

Careful! Rabbits like to hide in thorny bushes where they can't be reached.

Rabbits favor land with lots of natural cover so they can dive in quickly if danger approaches. Small bushes growing thickly together in a thicket, lots of blackberry canes or briars that form a fortress of sharp thorns, are where rabbits like to call home. They also seek areas with lots of tall grass and loose dirt where they can dig in their burrows to raise their young. These small animals will need to have a handy source of water nearby, so scout around for burrows built near water sources as well.

RABBITS LOVE FARMS AND FRESH VEGETABLES

Farmland, where crops grow, is another favorite place for rabbits. They lay low during the day and go out at night to feast on fresh vegetables, fruits, and grains. Not only will a rabbit eat beans growing in a field, but they will eat the leaves and stems of the plant as well. This destruction of crops makes the rabbit an enemy of farmers.

Rabbit droppings are distinctive. They look like small, round balls in a pile. These piles of droppings aren't hard to spot and can mean a rabbit or rabbit family is somewhere nearby. Search the bushes and briars nearby for bits of fur caught on the twigs and thorns for further evidence.

Wild rabbit droppings are distinctive round balls often found in a pile.

Rabbits also like to chew on things. Look for bushes, tree bark, or a patch of grass or tasty clover that's been nibbled down. Patches of vegetation may be eaten down to the nub.

Just like people, groups of rabbits living in an area use the same pathways through the landscape when they travel. Look for little trails where the grass or other vegetation has been trodden down in a continuous line or small tunnels through the underbrush or tall grass. These trails are rabbit highways! Follow these paths to the source where the rabbits live.

USE YOUR EARS

When hunting, pay close attention to the sounds all around you. All nature is very sensitive to sound, and when danger approaches, birds, animals, and insects become suddenly silent. If you have ever heard frogs croaking in a pond, walked in that direction, and the frogs became suddenly quiet, this is a good example.

While you are hunting, if all sounds suddenly cease, pay close attention to what is happening around you. The silence could mean a dangerous animal is hiding nearby, so be careful.

HERE'S THE SKINNY ON SQUIRRELS

Squirrels live and raise their families in trees and come down to run around on the ground in search of food and water. They build **dreys** or nests out of leaves and twigs in the branches of high trees. In the autumn when the acorns fall from the trees, squirrels can be seen on the ground eating the acorns or other nuts and gathering food to store for winter. They are not hibernating animals, and you can hunt squirrels all year.

Squirrels build their nests high in the trees.

Even if you don't live in a rural area, you can probably look out of your window and see squirrels. They live everywhere in cities, towns, and the countryside. However, shooting squirrels with a gun is not permitted in suburban areas.

In suburbia, squirrels can be quite destructive because they chew up wood and other parts of a house and make nests in people's attics. Squirrels can chew up electrical wiring and thus cause power outages or a house fire. Many people consider the squirrel to be a nuisance animal.

SQUIRRELS ARE NOISY AND CURIOUS

The rabbit is a silent animal, rarely making sounds, but the squirrel is quite lively and known for the chattering sounds it makes. You can hear a squirrel, even if you can't see it, high in the branches of a tall tree in its natural habitat.

Squirrels are inquisitive creatures. If you frighten one and it runs up a tree, the squirrel will probably stop halfway and then turn and watch what you are doing. Some squirrels, especially the ones that live near people, lose their fearfulness of humans. They will allow a person to get close to them and not run away. If you do something a squirrel doesn't like, such as making a loud noise, they chatter loudly as if they are scolding you for disturbing them.

SQUIRRELS IN THE WILD

If you are looking for an area in the wild to hunt squirrels, scout around for the chewed-up shells of nuts, acorns, or seeds on the ground under the canopy of trees. Squirrels are messy eaters and throw bits of gnawed material all over the place.

Squirrels are messy eaters and will leave chewed up shells behind.

When tracking squirrels in the wild, look for places where they have gnawed on tree bark. Unlike rabbits that chew on tree bark close to the ground, a squirrel chews the bark higher up the side of a tree. They also rub the side of their head on the chewed bark to leave their scent to mark their territory. If you find a tree with gnawed bark and empty hulls of various nuts and wild grains underneath, you know squirrels are living nearby.

Squirrels are another small animal that poses little threat to a beginning hunter. However, make sure a squirrel is dead before you pick it up. They have very sharp teeth and can inflict a nasty bite. Squirrels also can carry rabies.

BIG GAME - TRACKING DEER

When summer comes to a close, hunters feel a growing excitement as deer season approaches. They dream of the day when they bag that huge buck with the giant rack of antlers.

Hunters often dream of bagging a whitetail buck like this one.

Deer live all over the United States and Canada in several types of habitats. These super adaptive animals also thrive in suburban areas where herds of them can be observed moving through neighborhoods. Some people even leave out food, such as dried corn, for the local deer.

Other people consider deer a nuisance because they eat all sorts of ornamental plants. In some parts of the country, deer feed on decorative plants and flowers in local parks and other public places. Like the rabbit, deer also do a lot of damage to growing crops of fruits and vegetables. Unlike the rabbit, a deer can jump high fences, so it's hard to control them.

DEER ON THE FARM

If you live near farmland, this could be a good place to start tracking deer. Deer can do massive damage to food crops, and some farmers hunt deer to protect their fields. Always get permission from the landowner first and don't trespass on anyone's land. When hunting on another person's land, make sure you have an adult with you and your parents always know your location.

Deer can often be found on farmland.

A big cornfield is an excellent place to start scouting for signs of deer. Deer love to eat corn, and a big cornfield is irresistible because the tall corn provides plenty of food and offers plenty of tall cover so the deer can hide while eating. Some deer will even take up residence in a large cornfield. Besides corn, deer will eat just about any other edible plant on a farm such as beans, tomatoes, and squash. They will even break open watermelons and pumpkins to munch on the insides.

Deer usually rest in beds during the day and come out at night to feed, especially on moonlit nights. When scouting for deer signs, try to track them to their beds. Mule deer that live in the northern part of North America make beds at the bases of big boulders out of the wind or in sagebrush. Whitetail deer further south make beds in tall grass, cornfields, and in the underbrush in a wooded area.

TRACKING DEER IN THE WOODS

Deer favor the woods of North America as a habitat because of the plentiful food to eat and thick undergrowth where they can hide or sleep undisturbed. In the autumn, when the acorns and hickory nuts fall from the trees, the deer gather in the woods to eat the nuts. The many other types of edible trees and plants in wooded areas also provide plenty of food for deer herds.

When scouting for deer signs, look for their favorite foods. Deer love honeysuckle, a fast-growing vine with sweet, honey-like flowers and also wild, non-poisonous mushrooms. These animals like to eat leaves and twigs from dogwood, poplar, maple, and the fruit of wild blackberries, plums, and crabapples. Anywhere you can find these trees and plants, you are likely to see deer tracks that you can follow.

When looking for deer, look for their favorite foods.

LOOKING FOR DEER SCAT

Scat is animal feces or droppings. Deer scat consists of round, ball-like shapes usually found in a pile. Animals typically have a bowel movement soon after eating, so it's not unusual to see scat near a deer feeding site. Looking for scat helps a hunter to track more efficiently because each animal has unique-looking droppings. You can tell a lot about an animal from the appearance of the scat.

Deer scat provides a hunter with a great deal of information.

Large droppings come from a large, full-grown deer. The animal could be a big buck or even a large doe. A younger buck or a doe produces smaller droppings than a large animal. The smallest scat comes from a baby deer or fawn. If you find fawn droppings, this means there is a family of deer or a herd nearby as well.

If deer droppings are dry-looking and pale in color, this means they are not fresh. The deer is probably no longer in the area. If you see scat that's wet and moist, however, the deer could be nearby.

Some animals can be hard to track because of the strategies they employ to elude their prey. Deer, for instance, take huge bounds through the air when running from a dangerous threat which leaves fewer tracks and makes it harder for a hunter to follow their trail.

Raccoons are very cunning animals and know a lot of tricks to throw a hunting dog off their trail. When being chased by a dog, a raccoon will climb halfway up a tree, then leap off and land further away. This maneuver confuses the dog and convinces them the raccoon is still in the tree. The dog doesn't realize the wily raccoon has tricked them. Raccoons will also walk in a stream or creek to confuse a hunting dog. Water masks the scent of the animal so the dog can't track the raccoon.

Rabbits also have strategies to protect them from danger. One of their best protective measures is simply to freeze in place. Remaining motionless allows the rabbit to blend in with the surrounding landscape. Hiding in full view can be surprisingly effective.

Deer scat can also reveal what the animal has been eating. If you know what the animal has eaten, you can figure out where it has been spending its time. For example, if you see corn in the scat and there is a nearby cornfield, you know that's where the deer has been spending its time. This valuable information will help you track the movement of the deer before you begin hunting.

LOOK FOR DEER RUBS

You can't miss a deer rub. It looks like most of the bark has been scraped away from one spot on the side of a tree. If you know what to look for, deer rubs can yield a lot of valuable information to the young hunter—just like examining deer scat.

Male deer or bucks are responsible for the deer rubs found in the wild. Alpha bucks that lead a herd will rub their antlers on certain trees to mark their territory and warn away other male deer. Over time, big chunks of the bark can be rubbed off.

Large rubs with most of the bark scraped away indicate a big buck is in the area. The last part of October is usually the time of year when the bucks begin to rub the trees.

Deer rubs like this one can help you find your prey.

FOLLOW THE DEER TRAILS

Deer like to follow specific paths through the landscape just like other animals, such as rabbits. They usually favor walking in areas just on the edge of woods where they can quickly dart into cover if needed. Deer also like to travel through deep ditches and ravines where they can stay mostly out of sight. They'll follow trails along rows of large bushes, fences, or large trees that will offer cover, especially if near a body of water, such as a stream or river.

Deer need water to drink so track them near a stream when possible. Deer like to hide in the bushes and other vegetation that grows near water so look for signs of scat or rubs in these areas.

DID YOU KNOW?

Native Americans perfected the art of tracking and hunting animals because their lives and families depended on it. Men painted their faces and even clothing with different colors of clay and soot from fires as camouflage while hunting, or they would cover themselves with the skin of an animal. Native Americans also learned how to move silently through the woods so animals couldn't detect their presence.

Native Americans believed that all animals were sacred, and they wasted nothing when harvesting an animal. They preserved meat for future eating and made clothing and shoes from the animal's hide. From the tanned skins, they also made waterproof containers, blankets to keep warm, and baskets for storage. From horns, feathers, and claws, they made jewelry and ceremonial items.

Native Americans used every part of the animal, such as the hide, to make shoes like these beaded moccasins with leggings from the Lakota Sioux.

Native Americans knew how to watch animals for signs concerning the weather. When the animals built extra-thick dens in the autumn, the Native American knew this meant the winter would be extra harsh. The tribe would then gather extra food to store for the winter. The tribes knew that birds and other animals became very agitated before a big storm and understood this was a sign to take shelter.

TEXT-DEPENDENT QUESTIONS:

1.What kind of land do rabbits favor for their habitat?

2. Why is a farm a good place to track deer?

3. What is scat and what sort of information can a hunter derive from examining this substance?

RESEARCH PROJECT:

A good project to help the beginning hunter judge the age of tracks is to build a "track patch." It's best to start this project during dry weather.

To build the patch, you will need to clear a space of ground by removing all sticks, leaves, and rocks. Rake the ground well to break up any dirt clod or pull out any more embedded rocks. Leave the soil to settle overnight.

The next day, go out to your patch and with a stick or other pointed object for a tool, make five scratches into the soil. Use different amounts of pressure with each mark, from the lightest to the heaviest. After making the scratches study them carefully. Notice how the dirt edges are sharp and well defined.

Wait four to five hours and come back with your stick and make another five scratches in the soil beside the first ones. Study both sets of scratches carefully. See how the second scratches look much fresher and more defined. What do you notice about the first scratches?

Repeat this process with another set of five scratches four to five hours later. Notice how the first set of scratches and the second set no longer look fresh-made. The soil has begun to settle. Study the scratches carefully and observe how they have changed over time.

If you repeat this exercise in different seasons and different weather conditions, you will learn a lot about how to tell the age of a track. This valuable skill can make you a more successful hunter.

Write a paper on what you have learned from this project, or better yet, start a hunting journal where you can record your findings and refer back to them in the future.

 Words to Understand:

camouflage: To blend into the environment.

flush: To drive an animal or bird out of its hiding place and into the open.

foliage: The collective plant material.

CHAPTER 2
HUNTING STRATEGIES

The objective when hunting rabbits is to catch sight of them before they see you. For the young hunter, sneaking up on rabbits will give you the best advantage and the best aim for shooting. However, rabbits are assisted by nature when it comes to **camouflage**, and they aren't easy to see in the wild. They blend in very well with the surrounding landscape.

PLACES TO FIND RABBITS

To find where rabbits hide in the wild, go out driving with your parents in a rural area around sunset or sunrise. Rabbits are the most active during these two times, and you may see them hopping alongside roads near thickets or woods. Take note of the location and check with the landowner to see if you and an adult can obtain permission to hunt in that spot.

Rabbits like to live in neglected places that are close to human habitats. The long grass and overgrown weeds surrounding old barns and abandoned sheds are places where rabbits nest

A rabbit's habitat is the perfect camouflage.

and sleep because the smell of nearby humans keeps away many of their predators such as bobcats, coyotes, wild dogs, or foxes.

If you spot rabbit activity around old barns or sheds, always ask a parent to request the landowner's permission to hunt in that location. Be respectful and never leave litter or build fires on the property. It's also a nice gesture to be courteous and thank the landowner afterward for allowing you to hunt the rabbits.

Wildlife Tracking Basics

FIND THE FOOD SOURCE, FIND THE RABBITS

Rabbits look for locations that offer the most plentiful food sources. Someone's backyard vegetable garden, a fruit orchard, or a farm offers lots of tasty treats for a rabbit's midnight dinner. The sneaky cottontails wait until nightfall when the family dog is fast asleep to sneak in and eat all their little bellies can hold.

Rabbits will also make their homes where wild sources of food are available, such as blackberry thickets, native blueberries shrubs, or patches of strawberries. Rabbits also make their homes in spots that offer plenty of fresh grass or clover to eat.

FLUSHING OUT RABBITS

Well-trained hunting dogs can help flush out prey.

In an area where you have found lots of signs of rabbit activity, flushing out the rabbits is the next step. If you are hunting with dogs, let them catch a scent of a rabbit nearby. The dogs will run through briars and underbrush too thick for a human and **flush** out any rabbits hiding there. If you are not hunting with dogs, it's a bit trickier to flush out the cottontails.

When walking through long grass, don't walk in a straight line. Weave back and forth in a zigzag pattern. Walking in this manner alarms the rabbit, possibly because they think more than one predator is coming toward them. Be prepared with your gun, because any rabbits close by will suddenly shoot out of their hiding places.

Rabbits don't like to leave the comfort of their home base, so when flushed out of hiding they will run away from their pursuer, but then stop and wait to see what happens. Eventually, they circle back around to their home base. How far the rabbit will run before circling back depends on many factors, and it's hard to judge correctly. However, know the rabbit will appear again and be ready to shoot.

When hunting with dogs, always be careful when shooting. You don't want to hit the dog instead of the rabbit. If a dog is running too close behind the rabbit for you to make a safe shot, don't shoot.

STANDING STILL WORKS TOO!

Sometimes you can flush out a rabbit just by standing still. Here's how to do it.

Walk through an area of low brush or tall grass and make as much noise as you like to get a cottontail's full attention. Then come to a dead stop and just stand there silently not moving a muscle. Sometimes this maneuver tricks a rabbit into thinking you've spotted it and it will quickly dart from its hiding place. Be ready to shoot quickly when this happens because rabbits can move incredibly fast and you can easily miss the shot if you are not prepared.

If this strategy doesn't work the first time during a hunt, keep repeating the maneuver until you flush out a rabbit. It's best to try this silent flushing in a place where you have seen plenty of signs of rabbit activity such as scat or chewed vegetation.

TRACKING AND HUNTING SQUIRRELS

Hunting squirrels can be excellent training for the beginning hunter, especially hunting squirrels that live in rural areas. These woodland squirrels are warier and don't venture as close to humans as their city cousins do. Urban squirrels learn to tolerate the presence of people from an early age and aren't particularly nervous around people.

Squirrels are very quick and very observant like deer. Their large, dark eyes can detect the slightest movement in their surroundings, and they possess very keen hearing. The smallest sound attracts their attention, and like little acrobats, it only takes them a moment to swing from a tree limb and disappear into hiding.

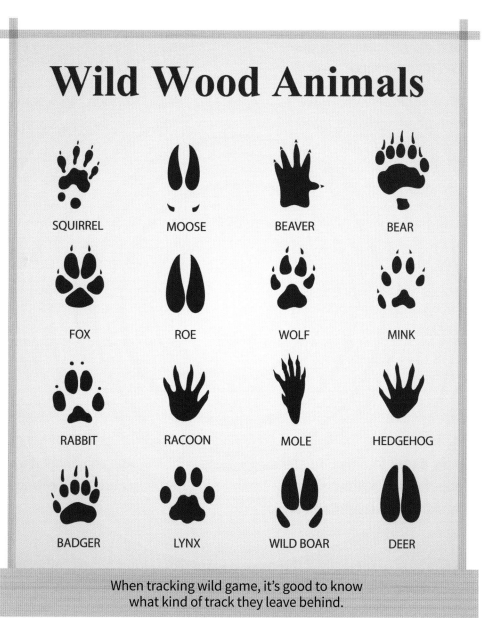

Wild Wood Animals

SQUIRREL   MOOSE   BEAVER   BEAR

FOX   ROE   WOLF   MINK

RABBIT   RACOON   MOLE   HEDGEHOG

BADGER   LYNX   WILD BOAR   DEER

When tracking wild game, it's good to know
what kind of track they leave behind.

Like rabbits, squirrels have periods of peak activity that coincide with sunrise and sunset. Early in the morning and late in the evening before the sun goes down is the best time for hunting squirrels.

Before your hunt, scout wooded areas for signs of squirrel activity, such as little piles of chewed shells of acorns and hickory nuts on the forest floor. Squirrels will also eat other foods such as seeds, grains, insects, and wild fruits such as muscadine grapes, blackberries, and persimmons. Pine seeds are also a favored food.

When on a squirrel hunt, move as silently as possible through the wooded area. Woodland squirrels try to avoid humans, and if they sense your presence or hear you walking past, they will quickly hide from sight. Located up in the tops of trees, you won't even detect their presence. The only thing you might see is a sudden flash of gray.

Wild squirrels are very active in the autumn when the acorns and other nuts fall from the trees. Squirrels get busy gathering these nuts, eating their fill, and burying the rest for the lean winter months ahead. If you enter the woods at this time of year looking for squirrels, listen for the sounds they make in the trees, such as chattering to one another and leaping back and forth in the tree branches.

SQUIRREL HUNTING STRATEGIES

The best way to hunt and bag a wild squirrel is to be patient, watch, and wait, like in deer hunting. Find a location with plenty of squirrel signs, then pick a spot under a tree to sit as quietly as possible until the squirrels think it's safe to move about again. When you hear them begin to rustle about in the trees, get ready to sight your target and shoot.

It's not the easiest thing to shoot a squirrel while looking up through the dense **foliage** of a tree, especially if the animal is rushing along a tree limb. Don't get anxious or in too much of a hurry. Take your time and aim as carefully as you can before firing. Make as little noise as possible.

Hunt for squirrels by waiting patiently and quietly in the woods.

If you miss your squirrel target, just remain as still as you can, wait about ten minutes, aim, and fire again. If you do hit a squirrel the second time, don't move from your spot and give away your presence and location. Just wait until the squirrels resume their activity in the tree and shoot again.

You can harvest many squirrels in this manner, without frightening the others. It will take time for the squirrels to realize something is wrong and run away and hide. In the meantime, you can make multiple kills.

USING A DEER STAND

Using a deer stand while hunting is one of the best tools for a young hunter. When perched in a deer stand, you cannot only sit comfortably and quietly, you can observe wildlife from an elevated position. You can even shoot a deer without leaving the stand.

When purchasing a deer stand, shop carefully. Ask for advice from older, more experienced hunters on the type of deer stand that is the best for your weight and height.

Young hunters need a deer stand that is easy to erect and also safe to use. Some hunters prefer to build their stands out of wood. Some deer stands can be very elaborate with sides and a roof while others are nothing but a piece of plywood mounted up in a tree.

To build your deer stand, start by scouting the area for signs of deer activity. You will want to construct your stand as close to the routes that deer travel for the greatest chance of success. Do your research and scout an area first. If you build your stand where there is little or no signs of deer activity, you will be wasting your time.

Choose sites for your stand that are close to a supply of water. When deer come to get a drink, you can take aim and fire from the deer stand.

A deer stand is an excellent place to wait for your prey.

THE WIND IS NOT YOUR FRIEND

While out hunting, a young hunter must be aware of the direction the wind is blowing. Be careful not to face a direction where the wind blows your scent toward your prey. When this happens, the wind will carry your scent and warn the animals you are in the vicinity.

Animals that live near humans, such as deer in an urban area, may not react as strongly to the human scent as deer living in a more rural setting where they do not encounter people very often. Animals that live near humans are wary of an approaching person, but they don't usually run away in terror unless chased.

Deer in the wild usually run away when they smell human scent. These animals view humans as predators.

SNOW CAN HELP WITH TRACKING

Snow can be a great help when tracking your prey.

In the areas of North America that receive snow for most of the winter season, tracking can be a lot easier. Deer tracks and droppings can be highly visible in the snow, and a hunter can easily follow a deer trail. However, a young hunter should be careful of freezing temperatures when hunting in the snow to avoid frostbite and hypothermia.

When snow hunting, it helps to wear snow camouflage when tracking deer. Deer have very keen eyesight and can detect movement from a far distance. The whiteness of snow makes the darker colors of clothing stand out starkly and makes a hunter more visible to deer.

Deer can also see quite well in the dark, which is helpful for feeding at night. Deer traditionally like to go on foraging missions on nights when the moon is full.

DID YOU KNOW?

In recent years it's a common sight to see deer in urban areas. Deer populations have been rapidly expanding all across the United States and Canada. Even in England, the deer populations have exploded. It's common to see deer walking through local parks, golf courses, on the side of roads, and in one's very own backyard.

When deer live alongside humans, they don't encounter as much danger from their natural predators as they do in the wild. The presence of people keeps the deer safe, and they can multiply freely with a stable food supply from lawns and other landscape plants.

Some people love the deer living in their neighborhood and regularly put out food such as dried corn, fresh vegetables, and fruit for the creatures. Other people are irritated because the animals eat expensive landscaping plants and occasionally jump out in front of cars and cause accidents. In some neighborhoods, it's not uncommon to see a small herd of deer strolling across the front lawn nibbling grass and taking a leisurely drink from a fish pond or birdbath.

In some places, seeing wild animals in town is a common sight.

Some communities across North America have protested against the large amounts of deer living in their area and want them removed. However, many more people support the idea of letting deer continue to live with humans undisturbed. They don't care if their rose bushes get nibbled because they love the sight of a live herd of deer in their yard!

Deer aren't the only ones that have adopted the advantages of urban living. Wolves and foxes have begun living among humans in parts of Europe, and mountain lions are living in Los Angeles. In Italian cities, wild boars frequently raid garbage cans for food and grow fat and sleek.

As the natural habitats of wild animals shrink, the creatures begin to move in alongside humans and adapt to a new way of living. They enjoy an ample supply of food in urban areas and protection from their predators.

TEXT-DEPENDENT QUESTIONS:

1. What should you do if you want to hunt on another person's land?

2. How are woodland squirrels different from squirrels that live in an urban area?

3. Why should you be careful of the direction of the wind while hunting?

RESEARCH PROJECT:

Begin this project by starting a tracking and hunting journal. When you go out scouting for spoor, keep a written record of your finds. Later when you go hunting, record how accurate your findings were in locating the habitats of animals.

At the end of the hunting season, compare all of your written journal entries to see how successful you were at tracking the animals you hunted. Determine your success percentage.

Be sure to test several methods of tracking and accurately record the results. Ask older, more experienced hunters for tracking tips they have used with success in the past. Test these methods while you are on hunting trips and record the results as well.

Write a three-page paper on the results. What tracking methods worked the best? Which ones worked the least? Be sure and fully explain your findings and opinions why some methods worked better than others.

Present your findings to other hunters and ask for their opinion. Did they have the same success rate as you did with certain tracking methods or did they experience different results? Write all their opinions in your hunting journal as well.

Don't throw away the journal! Keep it for future reference and keep expanding its contents as time passes. The journal will provide a valuable record of past hunts that you can study to grow as a successful hunter.

 Words to Understand:

flock: A group of birds.

gobble: One of the sounds a turkey makes.

roosting: The pattern of birds sleeping in trees at night to avoid predators.

CHAPTER 3
TRACKING AND HUNTING BIRDS

When tracking a wild animal, it's important to understand the animal's habits and food preferences. Having this specific knowledge helps a young hunter to know where to look for animals or birds. For instance, you wouldn't find many wild turkeys in a location with no trees because they need a place to roost at night.

Watch for these particular bird prints to help find your prey.

TRACKING TURKEYS

Turkeys prefer foraging on open land without a lot of trees, but they do require some trees to roost safely at night. If a **flock** of turkeys tried to roost on the ground, they would be attacked by animals in their sleep and killed. These birds usually follow a routine for sleeping. They roost in the same place every night, and you need to find out where those **roosting** trees are located to harvest the birds.

Art of
Stalking Tom
Brown III

LOOK FOR DROPPINGS

If you notice turkeys in a particular area, you will need to scout around to find where they are roosting. Turkeys roost together like chickens, and they usually pick the tallest tree in the area. Where you find one turkey, you will also find several more in the flock.

Searching around under trees for turkey droppings can indicate which trees the birds are roosting in at night. If you find droppings under trees, make sure they are fresh and moist and not old and dried. Fresh dropping means a turkey has roosted in the tree recently. Take note of the tree's location and come back later just before it gets dark to check if any turkeys are flying up to roost.

If turkeys are using that tree as a roosting spot, you can go home and prepare for your turkey hunt. When hunting turkeys, you will need to get up early and go back to the tree you scouted earlier before the sun rises. You will be able to see the turkeys as they come down from the trees.

Turkeys stay in flocks for protection.

TURKEYS LEAVE OTHER SIGNS

Turkeys leave very distinctive tracks in the soft dirt, mud, or even snow. They also scratch up the ground like chickens looking for food. Large flocks of turkeys can disturb large patches of leaves or soil looking for bug larvae and seeds, and this is what to look for when tracking these birds.

You should also scout for food sources. Turkeys like to eat wild blackberries, muscadine grapes, hickory nuts, beechnuts, and acorns. These large birds also enjoy eating grasshoppers and other bugs as well as wild grains found in long grass and open areas.

Turkeys make a very distinctive sound called a **gobble** as well as other noises. When scouting for turkeys in the wild, pay attention to any sounds the birds make. Then you will be able to identify a turkey sound when you hear it again.

FINDING PLACES TO HUNT TURKEYS

When searching for a place to hunt turkeys ask a parent to help you look online for public hunting areas in your part of the country. Hunting for turkeys is allowed in many places on state and federally owned land in the United States. Ask your parents to check with state wildlife agencies or with your local government for places to hunt on public land.

TURKEYS CHANGE LOCATIONS

When you go out scouting and tracking before your actual turkey hunt, make sure you don't let too much time lapse. Turkeys occasionally change locations because of food availability. You don't want to find a roosting tree only to return a few weeks later to hunt and all the turkeys have moved on to a new location.

Like many other animals, turkeys don't stay in one place for long.

EXAMINING SCAT FOR CLUES

Animal scat or bird droppings can yield a lot of clues that can help you when tracking or hunting. If you examine scat carefully, you will be able to determine what the creature has been eating recently. If you know what a rabbit had for its dinner, for example, you can figure out where it has been spending its time. Does the rabbit scat contain a lot of acorns? That means it has been in a wooded area nearby. Start tracking in the nearest wooded area and scout for more rabbit signs of activity in that location.

You can use this method of examining the scat for all animals and birds. It is one way to determine an animal's favorite haunts and hiding places. Be sure and examine fresh scat that will give you clues to the most recent activity. Older, dried-out scat may tell you what an animal has eaten, but it will be days or weeks ago, and the knowledge will be of little use to the hunter.

If you want to pull apart scat for a closer examination to determine what the animal has been eating, you should use a tree branch. Don't ever use your bare hands because you will risk exposure to harmful bacteria that can make you sick.

Use binoculars to scout for ducks in their natural environment.

SCOUTING FOR DUCKS

When scouting for ducks, you will need a good pair of binoculars. Drive around near waterways and swampy areas with a parent or other adult at the beginning of your search. If you see a single duck or several birds flying overhead, watch them through the binoculars and try to determine the direction from which they are coming or going. You will get a rough idea of where the ducks are hiding.

Some duck hunters go out in boats before hunting season starts to search for duck hideaways. They travel close along the shorelines of lakes and rivers, watching the birds with binoculars. The very dedicated duck hunters hire planes and use GPS systems so they can fly overhead to search for these birds. While flying in an aircraft, the hunters can look down and see all the hidden places where the ducks have settled.

Some very successful hunters scout for good duck locations all year round. They continuously watch where the ducks are hiding and when they move to a different area. These hunters monitor food sources and find where the ducks build nests to raise their young. Tracking ducks are best done this way because the hunter will learn a lot about the behavior of the local birds and the remote places where they like to hide. When hunting season arrives, the hunter already knows where to find the ducks because of their year-round efforts at tracking.

PREPARING FOR THE HUNT

When preparing for a duck hunt, you need to find out where the ducks hide so you won't waste a lot of time searching. If you haven't had any luck watching from a car, go out into the wild with an adult and search the marshy areas, fields, and lakes for signs of duck activity. Ducks roost in trees at night like turkeys, so look for places where they sleep, and look for droppings underneath trees.

Ducks need food, so look for places where they have been feeding. This location is where you should hunt. If you attempt to hunt where ducks sleep, this will drive them from the area, and you will have to start your search all over again.

Hunt where ducks like to eat.

PRACTICE! PRACTICE! PRACTICE!

Before hunting ducks for the first time make sure to target practice beforehand because these birds are notoriously hard to hit. Ducks fly quickly up into the air and are out of gun range in a flash. This element of surprise and difficulty in hitting one's target makes duck hunting one of the most exciting for game hunters.

Skeet shooting with a shotgun is very similar to hunting for ducks. The clay piece flies into the air at the same angle a duck would fly up into the sky. If you are planning to go duck hunting, you should practice skeet shooting for several months in advance to give you a head start on the season.

One of the reasons beginning duck hunters miss shots in the wild is anxiety. Try to relax and don't get flustered when ducks appear suddenly, or you will miss shots. Take the time to aim well, and you will have more success.

TRACKING AND HUNTING DOVES

Doves have excellent eyesight, and you should wear some serious camo when tracking and hunting these birds. These commonly-found birds can distinguish natural shades of color from man-made ones and will quickly flee the scene when they spot a human. Hunting doves can be an exciting sport to pursue because it's difficult to bag one of these crafty birds.

Doves can be crafty prey.

Good places for dove hunting are near a source of water or in an open field of grassland or near farmland. Doves especially like cornfields where they can gorge themselves on corn and hide among the tall plants. They also like to eat sunflower and millet seeds. Between meals, doves can be seen perched in trees and on utility lines. Sometimes, you can spot doves on the ground scratching around in freshly turned soil looking for insects or seeds.

When scouting for doves, look for a mix of open fields with nearby trees. Doves will spend their days foraging for food, and when night falls, they roost in trees.

CREATE YOUR OWN DOVE HABITAT

When there are no nearby trees on available hunting land to attract doves, some hunters will create roosts for the birds by cutting down small trees in another area and relocating them. Hunters dig a hole for the trunk of the tree, then stand it upright in the hole to hold it firm. Even if the tree is dead, the doves will still roost in its branches at night.

If you want to build a dead-tree roost for doves, be sure to ask an adult to help you with the process. Trees can be very heavy for one person to handle.

Doves eat gravel or coarse sand to help with their digestive process. You can pour a bag of sand or gravel on the ground to attract the local doves to your hunting spot. They will come to eat the gravel or sand and most likely remain in the area for you to hunt. Corn, sunflower, and millet seeds sprinkled on the ground will also attract doves.

If you want to bait an area of land to attract doves for hunting, be sure to ask a parent to check with local hunting laws to make sure it is legal in your area. A good hunter always obeys all laws.

TIPS FOR DOVE HUNTING

When hunting doves, you must sit very quietly. Even if you are wearing camo, a wily dove can detect even small movements. Not only do you need to remain very still, but you also need to sit that way for a long time to convince the doves it's safe to venture within range. Once the birds are in range, you can shoot.

If you are hunting with a bird dog, make sure the canine knows how to lie still as well. Doves are wary of a dog's presence and will stay out of gun range if they spot one.

When hunting doves, make sure to avoid elevated positions, such as the top of a hill. You will have much better luck if you stay in low-lying areas where you will be less noticeable to the doves, and they will venture closer.

You can create a dove habitat and wait for them to come to you.

DID YOU KNOW?

Benjamin Vernon Lilly or Ben Lilly was a legendary tracker and hunter in the American Old West. Ben possessed an almost superhuman ability for killing ferocious animals such as huge grizzly bears and mountain lions. He also hunted and killed a pack of rogue grizzly bears that were terrorizing the people of a Mexican town and became a folk hero.

During his lifetime, Ben Lilly hunted all over the United States from as far north as Idaho down into Mexico and acted in the capacity of a wilderness guide for President Theodore Roosevelt. Roosevelt was so impressed with the hunting and tracking skills of Ben Lilly that he wrote a book about the man's amazing talents. Lilly became famous, and his reputation became legendary.

Responsible hunting helps maintain healthy animal populations.

Ben Lilly became famous for his skill for living off the land as well as his hunting ability. Witnesses attested to the fact that he slept in trees in all kinds of weather and armed only with a knife, killed big bears for food. Ben had a fondness for eating roasted bear and mountain lion meat because he believed it gave him special powers when hunting. Ben Lilly also worked for the United States government tracking and hunting predatory animals for pay.

TEXT-DEPENDENT QUESTIONS:

1. What foods do wild turkeys like to eat?

2. Why do you need lots of target practice before hunting ducks?

3. Why are doves a challenge for a hunter to shoot?

RESEARCH PROJECT:

Start your research project by doing an Internet search for doves so that you can identify them. Then you can practice attracting doves to your backyard. Purchase some dried sunflower seeds, corn, and millet. Each day put some of the grains in a waterproof container in your backyard.

Watch the container and see what sort of birds eat the seeds. Are there any doves? It may be a few days or a week before the doves come to the food.

If you need to attend school or leave your home for other reasons, you can set up a small, inexpensive wildlife camera to record while you are away. Review the camera footage and see if any doves have visited.

Experiment with different types of seeds and grains to see which food the doves in your area prefer. Which food source gets eaten the quickest? Does weather make a difference? Keep day-to-day notes on this project for ten days.

When ten days are over, write a paper documenting your findings. Present this paper to three experienced dove hunters. What are their opinions? Do they agree with your results or disagree? Record all information in your hunting journal.

 Words to Understand:

deciduous trees: Trees that lose their leaves in winter.

evergreen trees: Trees that stay green all year round.

quarry: Hunted animals; prey.

CHAPTER 4
REGIONAL HABITATS

Wild animals live all over North America, but there are three common factors needed to create a habitat. These factors are a source of water, plentiful food, and a place of shelter from predators and extreme weather. Where these three conditions exist in nature, there is bound to be plenty of wildlife.

MOUNTAINS

Steep terrain can make mountain hunting extremely challenging.

In remote areas of high elevation with water, there is plenty of wild game, but the hunting conditions can be rough. In the western part of the United States and Canada are the Rocky Mountains, and in the east, are the Appalachian Mountains, the Catskill Mountains, and the Adirondack Mountains. These eastern mountain ranges are much older than the Rocky Mountains and are covered with dense vegetation, including many deciduous trees.

In the Rocky Mountains, you will find pronghorn antelope, elk, big sheep, and mule deer for hunting. Some commercial hunting services in conjunction with local landowners provide hunting access on private land for a fee. This arrangement makes it easy for hunters to find a good place to camp and hunt. Use the Internet to search for commercial hunting services available in your area.

Hunting in the mountains can be harder than other areas because of the steep terrain. In the mountains, it can be tough to get close enough to your **quarry** to get a decent aim. The wind is also a major factor while hunting in the mountains because wind currents can carry your scent for longer distances.

Tracking - The Six Disciplines of Tracking.

WOODED AREAS

From the extreme northern part of the United States all the way north to the Arctic Circle, the winters are long, and the summers are short. These areas have some of the largest forests in the world called the Boreal Forests, named after the Greek god of the North Wind. These vast forests have extremely cold temperatures and heavy snowfalls for most of the year. Trees in these forests are mostly **evergreen trees** with a few deciduous trees. In these extensive forests live grizzly bears, wolves, elk, deer, caribou, and moose. You can also find the smaller game such as rabbits and grouse.

Some of the animals that live in the Boreal Forest hibernate in the winter, such as black bears, and many birds migrate south for the winter, such as ducks.

Many animals live in this region because of the sparse human population and the large amounts of water. There are lakes and rivers for fishing and vast stretches of marshland that provide a vast hunting ground for ducks and geese.

Tracking animals in these forests can be easy when there is snow in winter and damp ground in summer, but the frigid temperatures can make hunting dangerous for an inexperienced hunter. With such huge stretches of unpopulated land, it could also be easy to get lost without an experienced guide.

Pockets of forest exist throughout the eastern parts of North America. These areas usually have plenty of water, food for forage, and shelter for deer, rabbit, and squirrel. There are also big game animals, such as wild boar and black bears. Temperatures are more moderate in these regions, making them safer for the young hunter.

BEARS AND OTHER DANGEROUS ANIMALS

Chance bear encounters are another reason not to track or hunt alone. The more people in your group, the less chance of a bear encounter. Bears will typically avoid humans, especially if there are several of them.

The same rule applies with a bear as with feral dogs. Remain as calm as possible and avoid eye contact with the bear. Do not run, but back slowly away. Do not turn and run, or the bear will perceive you as escaping prey and will come after you. Some hunters carry pepper spray to use for bear encounters gone wrong. This spray can be more effective than shooting the animal because with a gun, you may miss a vital spot and only anger the bear.

PRAIRIES

The prairie houses several different types of game.

Wide open areas of rolling grassland and streams, dotted with pastures and farms, provide an excellent habitat for many types of wild animals. Whitetail deer, pheasants, and rabbits are plentiful in these areas.

The primary challenge with hunting on the prairie is the open spaces where you can see for long distances, making hunting with binoculars necessary. You need to spot your prey before they spot you and on the prairie, this can be difficult. Any little movement you make can alert your prey, plus the steady winds of the prairie can cause mishaps, such as a flap of clothing that frightens away your quarry.

Hiding in low spots in the landscape, such as a dip, can help you to keep a low profile from which to scout for deer and other animals.

DESERTS

In the southwestern United States lies the desert region. Although the desert doesn't have a lot of water, there is still wild game to be found here for tracking and hunting. One animal is the Coues deer; it's smaller than other types of deer, but able to survive in this arid environment.

Tracking or hunting in the desert involves keen survival skills, because not only is water in short supply, but poisonous spiders, snakes, and scorpions are plentiful. The landscape consists of sharp, spiny cactus and other plants that can make walking difficult. When the sun goes down, the temperatures can plummet dramatically, and the hunter needs to be prepared.

The beginning hunter should never venture out into the desert without an adult, especially if you are not accustomed to this type of environment.

The desert provides plenty of hunting.

When hunting in the desert, always make sure you have plenty of water, food, and a cell phone for emergencies.

FARMLANDS

Don't be afraid to hunt in farmland. Just ask for permission from the owners first!

Large fields of alfalfa, corn, or other vegetables are like big restaurants for many forms of wildlife such as deer and rabbits. If a source of water is nearby, deer will make their beds in the cornfields, hiding among the stalks and eating the corn. Rabbits will dig burrows in the dirt near fields and raise their young.

You must ask permission from the farmers to track or hunt on their land. However, this may not be difficult because some landowners are happy to let hunters shoot the wild animals that are eating their crops. Ask your parents to get permission for you and always hunt with an adult. Dogs may be helpful when hunting in large cornfields for rabbits.

WILD DOGS

Young hunters will encounter many surprises when tracking and hunting in the wild, and some of them can be quite dangerous. Feral dogs fall into this category. Some feral dogs were once domesticated, and others were born wild. These canines have nothing in common with gentle pets. These vicious dogs hunt in packs and have been known to attack and fatally wound humans.

If you encounter a pack of feral dogs while tracking or hunting, you should remain calm and try not to show any fear. Never run or turn your back on the dogs, or they will attack you. If you have a gun, you can shoot into the air to scare the dogs away, but if that doesn't work, you may have to shoot to defend yourself.

If you don't have a gun, your best bet may be to climb the nearest tree and wait until the dogs leave the area. If you can't make it to a tree, use the closest weapon to defend yourself such as a sharp stick or a good-sized rock.

The best strategy to deal with aggressive feral dogs is to carry pepper spray. This chemical will temporarily cause pain to the animal and allow you to escape unharmed. You can clip the pepper spray to your belt for easy access.

SWAMPS

All kinds of animals call swamps their home.

Swamps offer plenty of water for animals, and many types of wild game live in this habitat. Whitetail deer need plenty of water to drink and will usually visit a water source right after they wake from sleep.

Not only do deer like swamps because of the abundant water, they like to make their beds in the tall cattails that live near the water's edge. These tall plants provide the deer with plenty of cover to hide from predators.

When tracking along the edges of swamps, you can find signs of ducks, pheasants, raccoons, and deer. Be extra careful of poisonous snakes in swampland. In the southern region of the United States, you must also watch out for alligators. A young hunter should not track or hunt in swampy land alone. Take an adult with you for guidance and protection. Even older teen hunters should not hunt alone in swamps.

SOME CAUTIONS WHILE TRACKING

When out roaming through the wild and scouting for animal or bird tracks, be aware of several dangers you may encounter. By being aware of risks, you can take steps to minimize the threat of any problems, such as infectious disease.

TICKS

Ticks can pose a real threat to a young hunter's state of health. Ticks lurk almost everywhere in the wild just waiting to bite you for a meal of fresh blood. Tick bites are not only painful and unpleasant to remove from the skin, but they also can transmit some deadly diseases to humans. Lyme Disease and Rocky Mountain Spotted Fever are two of the most prevalent diseases spread by ticks in the United States and Canada. Unfortunately, there are no vaccines to prevent these illnesses.

Ticks can easily transfer from an animal to a human.

To protect yourself from being bitten by ticks, use spray-on tick repellent, especially one that contains the chemical permethrin. Spray all of your clothing and hunting gear as well. You don't want a tick to crawl into your backpack and hitch a ride home with you.

For good measure, tuck your pants into your boots or socks so ticks can't crawl up under your clothing and attach themselves to your skin. Once ticks have punctured the skin, they can transmit disease. Make sure your shirt is tucked inside of your pants as well to keep ticks away from your body. Wearing a hat or cap will help prevent ticks from crawling into your hair.

After a hunt, always take a hot shower and wash your hair with plenty of shampoo. If an unattached tick is in your hair, the shampoo will most likely kill it. After the hot shower, examine your body carefully for any ticks. Ask a parent to search your scalp and other places, such as your back and neck, that you can't see.

If you are hunting with dogs, make sure they are protected from ticks as well. Ask your parents to talk with a veterinarian about tick treatments for dogs. After each hunt, examine your dogs closely to make sure they haven't picked up any ticks in the wild. Remove ticks with a pair of tweezers and squish them! Be sure to wash your hands thoroughly afterward.

When you are field dressing deer or other animals, watch out that ticks don't detach themselves from your kill and crawl onto you. Keep a sharp lookout also while skinning animals and handling hides.

If bitten by a tick, you should let your parents know. If you develop a rash or fever within a time frame of three weeks after being bitten by a tick, be sure to tell your parents and seek medical attention. Prompt treatment is vital for recovery.

RABIES

All warm-blooded animals like this raccoon can transmit
rabies to humans with one bite.

Ticks are not the only ones that carry disease. All warm-blooded animals can transmit rabies to a human. If you are tracking in an area and encounter an animal that behaves strangely, such as staggering when walking or salivating so heavily that it drips from the animal's mouth, get away from that animal as fast as you can.

Wild animals that appear unusually friendly or not afraid of humans can be infected with rabies as well. Don't touch an animal if it approaches you in the wild. Move away as fast as you can.

You should always wear latex gloves when handling a dead animal, especially during field dressing and butchering meat. The rabies virus can enter a person's bloodstream through scratches or cuts on their hands. You should not eat or drink anything at this time as well. Wait until after you have removed your clothes and showered with hot water and plenty of soap. Then it will be safe to eat or drink.

If you shoot an animal that is behaving strangely, don't touch the carcass. It could be infected with rabies. If you are hunting with dogs, don't allow them near the dead animal.

POISON IVY

When scouting an area, don't forget to watch out for poison ivy. Some people are more allergic to this plant than others, but regardless, it can make you miserable and itchy.

Before going out in the wild, search the Internet for pictures of poison ivy. Once you know what to look for, you can steer clear of this plant. When tracking animals and searching for signs of animal or bird activity, take a few minutes and examine the surrounding vegetation if you need to push through shrubs or underbrush.

Watch out for poison ivy. As the saying goes,
"leaves of three; let them be."

One of the best ways to keep your skin safe from poison ivy is to keep your body covered with clothing. Wear lightweight long sleeve shirts and pants in summer when tracking through the woods or shrubby areas to protect yourself.

When you get back home, be sure to remove all the clothing you wore while tracking and wash it in hot water and detergent. Then take a hot shower and scrub yourself with plenty of soap. This action will remove any of the urushiol oil from the poison ivy that may have gotten on your skin.

If you suspect you might have brushed up against poison ivy while out tracking, be sure to wash the area well with hot water and soap when you get home. If home and a hot shower are not nearby, you can carry water in a canteen and soap in your backpack for this purpose. The water may not be hot, but with enough soap, you can remove the urushiol oil from your skin.

DID YOU KNOW?

Jim Corbett was a British officer born in 1875 who used his influence to create a national park for the protection of endangered Bengal tigers in India. However, he also hunted man-eating big cats to help protect the lives of local women and children.

When the Indian government asked for assistance, Corbett tracked and fatally shot the infamous Champawat Tiger that had killed over 400 people. Later, Corbett shot the Panar Leopard, another vicious animal that had cut short the lives of several hundred humans. He hunted and shot several other man-eating large cats throughout his lifetime.

It's estimated that the leopards and tigers Corbett stalked and killed had taken the lives of over 1,200 people.

The Jim Corbett National Park in India protects Bengal tigers.

TEXT-DEPENDENT QUESTIONS:

1. What's the best way for deterring a bear?

2. What do you do if bitten by a tick?

3. What is the best way to prevent poison ivy?

RESEARCH PROJECT:

List all the types of possible animal habitats in your area where you want to hunt. Make another list of all the wildlife you may encounter in those specific habitats. For example, if you wish to hunt in a wooded area, what animals are you likely to find while tracking or hunting?

Use a map to pinpoint the available food and water sources in that area. You can use this map later when tracking animals before a hunt. Enter this information into a hunting journal to keep handy for later reference.

Briars: A patch of thick underbrush that is full of thorny bushes. Rabbits and other small game love to hide in these.

Burrow: A hole made by a small animal where they live and stay safe from predators. It is also the word for what an animal does when it digs these holes.

Carcass: The dead body of an animal after the innards have been removed and before it has been skinned.

Field dress: To remove the inner organs from an animal after it has been harvested. It's important to field dress an animal as quickly as possible after it has been harvested.

Habitat: The area in which an animal lives. It's important to preserve animal habitats.

Hide: The skin of an animal once it has been removed from the animal. Hides can be made into clothing and other useful gear.

Homestead: A place or plot of land where a family makes their home. This is different from habitat because it is manmade.

Kmph: An abbreviation for kilometers per hour, which is a metric unit of measurement for speed. One kilometer is equal to approximately .62 miles.

Marsh: A wet area of land covered with grasses. The water in a marsh is often hidden by cattail, grasses, and other plants.

Maul: To attack and injure—either an animal or human being can be mauled.

Mph: An abbreviation for miles per hour, which is a unit of measurement for speed. One mile is equal to approximately 1.61 kilometers.

Pepper spray: A chemical used to repel bears and other dangerous creatures. It causes irritation and burning to the skin and eyes.

Poaching: The act of harvesting an animal at a time and place where it is illegal. Always follow the local hunting laws and regulations.

Process a kill: This is when an animal is butchered and cut up into pieces of meat to prepare for cooking. A kill can be processed by yourself or commercially.

Prey: Animals that are hunted for food—either by humans or other animals. It can also mean the act of hunting.

Roosting: What birds do when they rest upon a branch or a tree. Roosting keeps sleeping birds safe from predators.

Scout: To look ahead and observe an area. It is important to scout an area before hunting there. It helps you find evidence of your prey.

Suburbia: The area, people, and culture of a suburban, which is an area outside of a city or town where people live. It is often a small area full of houses.

Swamp: An area of wet land covered in grasses, trees, and other plant life. A swamp is not a good place to build a home, but it can be a good place to hunt.

Thicket: A collection of bushes and branches where small animals, like rabbits and rodents, like to hide.

Timid: A lack of confidence; shy. Rabbits, deer, and birds are often timid, which helps keep them alert and safe from predators.

Vegetation: All of the plant life in an area.

INDEX

FURTHER READING

Rezendes, Paul. *Tracking and the Art of Seeing: How to Read Animal Tracks and Sign.* Collins Reference; 2nd edition. 1999.

Elbroch, Mark. *Mammal Track and Sign: A Guide to North American Species. Stackpole* Books. 2003.

Brown, Tom. *Tom Brown's Field Guide to Nature Observation and Tracking.* Berkley. 1986.

Lowery, James. *Tracker's Field Guide: A Comprehensive Manual for Animal Tracking.* Falcon Guides. 2013.

Cheney, Cleve. *The Comprehensive Guide to Tracking: In-Depth Information on How to Track Animals and Humans Alike.* Safari Press. 2013.

INTERNET RESOURCES

www.rabbithuntingonline.com
An excellent site for information on tracking and hunting rabbits.

www.naturetracking.com
A good site for beginners with lots of photos of animal and bird tracks and information on tracking schools.

www.deeranddeerhunting.com
This site contains plenty of information on tracking and hunting deer.

www.acornnaturalists.com
This website provides very good information on tracking animals and birds of North America and tracking schools.

ORGANIZATIONS TO CONTACT

The National Shooting Sports Foundation
Flintlock Ridge Office Center
11 Mile Hill Road
Newton, CT 06470-2359
Phone: (203) 426-1320
Fax: (203) 426-1087
Internet: www.nssf.org

National Firearms Association
P.O. Box 49090
Edmonton, Alberta
Canada T6E 6H4
Phone: 1-877-818-0393
Fax: 780-439-4091
Internet: nfa.ca

The International Hunter Education Association
800 East 73rd Ave, Unit 2
Denver, Co 80229
Phone: 303-430-7233
Fax: 303-430-7236
Internet: www.ihea-usa.org

The National Wildlife Federation
11100 Wildlife Center Drive
Reston, VA 20190
Phone: 1-800-822-9919
Internet: www.nwf.org

PHOTO CREDITS

VIDEO CREDITS

Chapter 1
Tracking 101 - Black Scout Tutorials: http://x-qr.net/1D3B

Chapter 2
Wildlife Tracking Basics: http://x-qr.net/1Fug

Chapter 3
Art of Stalking: http://x-qr.net/1DAu

Chapter 4
Tracking - The Six Disciplines of Tracking: http://x-qr.net/1EUc

AUTHOR'S BIOGRAPHY

Elizabeth Dee has hunted extensively in the southeast part of the United States for small and large game. She has also cleaned and cooked game for family meals. Elizabeth has been writing for over 25 years for magazines and web articles.